Gioachino
ROSSINI

STABAT MATER

for Soli, Chorus and Orchestra
with Latin and English text

CHORAL SCORE

K 06398

STABAT MATER.

◆

No. 1.—INTRODUCTION.

CHORUS AND QUARTET.

Stabat mater dolorosa
Juxta crucem lacrymosa,
Dum pendebat Filius.

No. 2.—AIR.—(TENOR.)

Cujus animam gementem
Contristantem et dolentem
Pertransivit gladius.
O quam tristis et afflicta
Fuit illa benedicta
Mater Unigeniti;
Quæ mœrebat, et dolebat
Et tremebat, cum videbat
Nati pœnas inclyti.

No. 3.—DUET.—(1st & 2nd SOPRANO.)

Quis est homo qui non fleret
Christi matrem si videret
In tanto supplicio?
Quis non posset contristari
Piam matrem contemplari
Dolentem cum Filio?

No. 4.—AIR.—(BASS.)

Pro peccatis suæ gentis
Vidit Jesum in tormentis,
Et flagellis subditum.
Vidit suum dulcem natum
Morientem desolatum
Dum emisit spiritum.

No. 5.—RECITATIVE (BASS) AND CHORUS.

(Without Accompaniment.)

Eia, mater, fons amoris,
Me sentire vim doloris
Fac, ut tecum lugeam.
Fac ut ardeat cor meum
In amando Christum Deum,
Ut sibi complaceam.

No. 6.—QUARTET.

Sancta mater, istud agas,
Crucifixi fige plagas
Corde meo valide.
Tui nati vulnerati,
Tam dignati pro me pati,
Pœnas mecum divide.
Fac me vere tecum flere
Crucifixo condolere,
Donec ego vixero.
Juxta crucem tecum stare,
Te libenter sociare
In planctu desidero.
Virgo, virginum præclara,
Mihi jam non sis amara,
Fac me tecum plangere.

No. 7.—CAVATINA.—(2nd SOPRANO.)

Fac ut portem Christi mortem,
Passionis ejus sortem,
Et plagas recolere
Fac me plagis vulnerari,
Cruce hâc inebriari,
Ob amorem Filii.

No. 8.—AIR (1st SOPRANO) AND CHORUS

Inflammatus et accensus
Per te, Virgo, sim defensus
In die judicii.
Fac me cruce custodiri,
Morte Christi præmuniri,
Confoveri gratiâ.

No. 9.—QUARTET.

(Without Accompaniment.)

Quando corpus morietur,
Fac ut animæ donetur
Paradisi gloria.

No. 10.—FINALE.

In sempiterna sæcula. Amen.

TRIBULATION

No. 1.—INTRODUCTION.

CHORUS AND QUARTET.

Lord most holy! Lord most mighty!
Righteous ever are Thy judgments.
Hear and save us, for Thy mercies' sake.

No 2.—AIR.—(TENOR.)

Lord! vouchsafe Thy loving-kindness,
Hear me in my supplication,
  And consider my distress.
Lo! my spirit fails within me,
Oh! regard me with compassion,
  And forgive me all my sin!
Let Thy promise be my refuge,
Oh, be gracious and redeem me,
  Save me from eternal death!

No. 3.—DUET.—(1st AND 2nd SOPRANO.)

Power eternal! Judge and Father!
  Who shall blameless stand before Thee,
    Or who Thy dreadful anger fly!
Hear, and aid us strength to gather
  To obey Thee, still adore Thee,
    In hope and faith to die!

No. 4.—AIR.—(BASS.)

Through the darkness Thou wilt lead me,
In my trouble Thou wilt heed me,
  And from danger set me free.
Lord! Thy mercy shall restore me,
And the day-spring shed before me,
  All salvation comes from Thee!

No. 5.—RECITATIVE (BASS) AND CHORUS.

(*Without Accompaniment.*)

Thou hast tried our hearts towards Thee;
but if Thou wilt not forsake us, our souls shall
fear no ill.

Lord! we pray Thee, help Thy people;
save, O save them; make them joyful, and
bless Thine inheritance.

No. 6.—QUARTET.

I have longed for Thy salvation, and my
hope was in Thy goodness! Blessed be Thy
Name, O Lord, for ever!

Now and henceforth, we beseech Thee, turn
our hearts to Thy commandments, and incline
them evermore to keep Thy law.

Give Thy servants understanding, so that
they may shun temptation, and in all things
follow Thee.

Oh! vouchsafe us-true repentance, teach us
always to obey Thee, and to walk the way of
peace.

Let Thy light so shine before us,
And Thy mercy be upon us,
  Ev'n as is our trust in Thee.

No. 7.—CAVATINA.—(2nd SOPRANO.)

I will sing of Thy great mercy, for I was in
deep affliction, and Thou didst deliver me. I
will call unto the people, and the nations all
shall hear me, and shall praise Thy holy
Name!

No. 8—AIR (1st SOPRANO) AND CHORUS.

When Thou comest to the judgment, Lord,
remember Thou Thy servants! None else can
deliver us.

Save, and bring us to Thy kingdom, there
to worship with the faithful, and for ever dwell
with Thee!

No. 9.—QUARTET.

(*Without accompaniment.*)

Hear us, Lord! We bless the Name of our
Redeemer! and His great and wondrous
mercies now and ever glorify!

No. 10.—FINALE.

To Him be glory evermore. Amen.

Nº 1. Introduction.

Andantino moderato. (♪ = 132.)

Piano.

BELWIN MILLS PUBLISHING CORP.

PRINTED IN U.S.A.

4

6

mo - sa, dum pen - de - bat fi - li -
judg - ments: save us for thy mer - cy's

mo - sa, dum pen - de - bat fi - li -
judg - ments: save us for thy mer - cy's

us.
sake.

us.
sake.

ff Chorus.
Jux - - ta cru - - cem
Right - - eous ev - - er

ff Chorus.

ff Chorus.
Jux - - ta
Right - - eous

ff Chorus.
Jux - - ta cru - cem la - - cry -
Right - - eous ev - - er are thy

ff

12

Tenor Solo.

№ 2. Cujus animam.

(Lord, vouchsafe thy loving kindness.)

Air.

Allegro maestoso. (♩ = 100.)

14

per tran-si-vit gla-di-us.
and con-sid-er my dis-tress.

O quam tris tis et af -
Lo! my spir it fails with -

flic ta fu it il la
in me: Oh! re gard me

be ne dic ta, fu it
with com pas sion, Oh! re -

il la be ne dic ta
gard me with com pas sion,

Ma - - ter, Ma - - ter u - ni-ge - ni-
and_____ for - give,_____ for - give me all my

ti.
sin.
O quam tris - tis
Lo! my spir - it

et af - flic - ta fu - it
fails with - in me: Oh! re -

il la be - ne - dic - ta
gard me with com - pas - -sion,

Ma - - ter, Ma - - ter u - ni -
and for - give, for - give me

18

Nº 3. "Quis est homo."
(Power Eternal.)
Duet.

ho - mo / ter - nal!

qui non fle - ret, / Judge and Fa - ther!

Chris-ti ma - trem / Who shall blame - less

si vi- / stand be-

de - ret, / fore thee?

Chris-ti ma - trem / Who shall blame - less

si vi - de - ret / stand be-fore thee, or

in / Thy

22

Nº 4. "Pro Peccatis"

(Through the darkness.)

Air.

Allegretto maestoso. (♩ = 88.)

Pro___ pec - ca - tis su - ae___ gen - tis vi - dit
Through the_ darkness thou___ wilt lead me, In___ my

sotto voce.

Je - sum in___ tor - men - tis, et___ fla - gel - lis
troub-le thou___ wilt heed me, And___ from dan - ger

Nº 5. "Eia mater."
(Thou hast tried our hearts.)
Chorus and Recitative.

36

Andante mosso.

Nº 6. "Sancta mater, Istud agas.
(I have longed for thy Salvation.)
Quartet.

44

46

48

Nº 7. "Fac ut portem."

(I will sing of thy great mercy.)

Cavatina.

sor - tem et pla - gas re - co - le - re,
flic - tion, and thou didst de - liv - er me,

et _____ pla - gas
Lord, _____ thou didst

re - - - - - - - co' - le - re.
de - - - - - - - liv - er me!

59

Nº 8. "Inflammatus et accensus."
(When thou comest.)
Air and Chorus.

72

No 9. "Quando corpus."
(Hear us, Lord.)
Quartet (without accompaniment.)

Nº 10. "In sempiterna saecula, Amen."

(To Him be Glory evermore.)

Chorus.

(The four Solo parts with the Chorus.)

men, in sem-pi-ter - na
to him be glo - ry
men, in sem-pi-
to him be
men,
sae - - cu - la, A
ev - - er - more,
ter - na sae - - cu - la, A -
glo - ry ev - - er-more,
in sem-pi - ter - na sae - - cu-
to him be glo - ry ev - - er-
in sem-pi - ter - na sae - cu - la,
to him be glo - ry ev - er - more,
cresc.
f
ff
men, A
men, A
la, A
more,
A - men,
ff

Tempo I. Animato.

Tempo I. Animato.